FHA Loan Myths, Mistakes & Borrower Strategies

What Most Buyers Get Wrong—and How Smart Borrowers Win with FHA Loans

By Joseph G. Correa

Licensed Mortgage Broker, Finibi Mortgage

Copyright & Legal Notice

Published by Live Stronger Faster

First Edition, 2026

Table of Contents

Foreword

For many people, the idea of homeownership feels confusing, intimidating, or even unreachable—not because they lack income or responsibility, but because they have been surrounded by misinformation, half-truths, and outdated beliefs about how mortgage lending really works. Few loan programs have been misunderstood more than FHA loans. Over the years, FHA has been labeled as a "last resort," a "weak buyer loan," or something only meant for people in financial trouble. These myths have caused countless borrowers to delay buying a home, miss wealth-building opportunities, or accept loan terms that were never in their best interest. This final book in *The FHA Homeownership & Wealth Series* exists to clear the fog, correct the record, and empower borrowers with the truth—so they can use FHA loans strategically, confidently, and intelligently.

Throughout this series, you have learned how FHA loans work, who qualifies, how to buy a first home, how to overcome credit challenges, how self-employed borrowers can get approved, how to finance non-perfect properties, how to manage down payments and closing costs, how to refinance, how to access equity, and how to use FHA loans to purchase multi-unit properties and build long-term wealth. This final book brings everything together by addressing the most common mistakes borrowers make—not because they are careless, but because no one ever explained the system clearly. FHA loans are not designed to trap borrowers; they are designed to open doors. When used correctly, they can be one of the most powerful financial tools available to everyday Americans.

One of the biggest myths this book will dismantle is the idea that FHA loans are inferior to conventional loans. In reality, FHA loans were created to serve a different purpose. They are designed to provide flexibility, accessibility, and opportunity—especially for buyers who are early in their financial journey, rebuilding credit, self-employed, or navigating non-traditional income paths. FHA loans are not a sign of weakness; they are often a sign of strategic thinking. Many financially savvy borrowers intentionally choose FHA loans even when they qualify for other programs, because they understand leverage, liquidity, and long-term planning. This book will show you how those borrowers think—and how you can adopt the same mindset.

Another widespread mistake borrowers make is assuming that once they are "approved," their job is done. Approval is only the beginning. Smart borrowers understand that the loan they choose today affects their cash flow, equity position, refinancing options, and investment potential for years to come. FHA loans are especially powerful when viewed as part of a long-term plan rather than a one-time transaction. Whether your goal is stability, flexibility, or future investment, this book will help you align your mortgage decisions with your bigger financial picture. FHA loans can be stepping stones, launchpads, or long-term solutions—depending on how they are structured and used.

This book also confronts one of the most damaging myths in real estate: that waiting is safer than buying. Many borrowers delay purchasing a home because they believe they need perfect credit, more savings, or better timing. In reality, time is often the most expensive factor. Rising home prices, rent increases, and lost equity compound far faster than most people realize. FHA loans were specifically designed to help buyers enter the market sooner—not recklessly, but responsibly. By understanding FHA rules, compensating factors, and lender overlays, borrowers can often qualify earlier than expected without taking unnecessary risks. This book will help you distinguish between smart preparation and unnecessary delay.

Mistakes with FHA loans are rarely about eligibility—they are usually about execution. Borrowers choose the wrong lender, misunderstand debt-to-income ratios, misuse credit before closing, fail to plan for mortgage insurance, or miss opportunities to refinance at the right time. These mistakes are avoidable when borrowers understand how lenders think, how underwriters evaluate risk, and how FHA guidelines are actually applied in real-world scenarios. This book pulls back the curtain on the lending process so you can move from being a passive applicant to an informed participant. Knowledge is not just power in mortgage lending—it is leverage.

One of the most important themes in this book is strategy. FHA loans reward borrowers who think ahead. Whether it is choosing a property with future rental potential, structuring a cash-out refinance for reinvestment, or using FHA as a bridge to conventional financing later, smart borrowers use FHA rules to their advantage. This book is not about gaming the system—it is about understanding it. FHA guidelines are publicly available, but few borrowers are taught how to interpret them in a way that benefits their long-term goals. By the time you finish this book, you will understand not only what FHA allows, but why those rules exist and how to work within them intelligently.

This final volume also addresses fear—fear of denial, fear of making the wrong decision, fear of committing to a mortgage, and fear of being "stuck." These fears are common and understandable, especially for first-time buyers or those who have experienced financial setbacks. FHA loans were created during a time of economic hardship to restore confidence in homeownership. That mission still exists today. When borrowers are educated, prepared, and strategic, FHA loans can provide stability rather than stress. This book aims to replace fear with clarity, confusion with confidence, and hesitation with informed action.

As you read this book, you will notice that the focus is not just on what to avoid, but on how to win. Winning with FHA loans does not mean stretching beyond your means or chasing unrealistic expectations. It means understanding the rules, choosing the right professionals, planning ahead, and using the loan as a tool rather than a crutch. It means recognizing that homeownership is not just about buying a house—it is about building a foundation for financial growth, flexibility, and security. FHA loans can be part of that foundation when used intentionally.

This book is also a reminder that FHA loans are not just for buying a first home—they can be part of a lifelong financial strategy. Many borrowers start with FHA, refinance into conventional loans, leverage equity, purchase additional properties, or use FHA again later in life under different circumstances. There is no single "right" path, only informed choices. The goal of this book is to equip you with the mindset and knowledge to make those choices confidently, no matter where you are in your journey. As the final book in *The FHA Homeownership & Wealth Series,* this volume serves as both a conclusion and a bridge. It reinforces the lessons learned throughout the series while preparing you to take real-world action. FHA loans are not perfect—but no loan program is. What matters is how well the loan aligns with your goals, your timeline, and your financial reality. When myths are replaced with facts and mistakes are replaced with strategy, FHA loans become exactly what they were intended to be: a powerful pathway to homeownership and wealth for everyday people.

If this book does its job, you will never look at FHA loans the same way again. You will see opportunity where others see limitation, strategy where others see confusion, and possibility where others hesitate. And most importantly, you will be equipped to make decisions that serve not just your present needs, but your future goals. That is the true purpose of this book—and the reason this series ends not with rules, but with clarity.

Chapter 1

The FHA Myth Trap: Why Smart Borrowers Win While Others Wait

One of the most damaging forces in the homeownership journey is not bad credit, low savings, or even high interest rates—it is misinformation. Over the years, FHA loans have become surrounded by myths that quietly sabotage borrowers before they ever apply. These myths are often repeated by friends, family members, real estate agents, online forums, and even professionals who do not fully understand FHA guidelines. As a result, many qualified buyers delay buying a home, choose the wrong loan, or believe they must be in a "perfect" financial position before taking action. The truth is that FHA loans were never designed for perfection; they were designed for progress.

The first and most common myth is that FHA loans are only for borrowers who are financially desperate or irresponsible. This belief could not be further from reality. FHA loans were created to expand access to homeownership, not to label borrowers as high risk. In fact, many FHA borrowers have stable income, solid payment history, and long-term financial plans. What they may lack is a large down payment, a long credit history, or perfectly optimized debt ratios. FHA recognizes that these factors alone should not prevent someone from owning a home. The program is structured to evaluate borrowers holistically, not through a narrow, one-size-fits-all lens.

Another widespread myth is that FHA loans are more expensive than conventional loans and therefore should be avoided whenever possible. While FHA loans do include mortgage insurance, this cost must be evaluated in context. FHA often offers lower interest rates, more flexible approval standards, and higher allowable debt-to-income ratios. For many borrowers, especially first-time buyers, the ability to buy sooner with less money out of pocket far outweighs the perceived cost difference. Waiting years to save a larger down payment often results in higher purchase prices, increased rent costs, and lost equity—expenses that rarely get included in the comparison.

Many borrowers also believe that using FHA is a sign of poor financial planning. In reality, strategic borrowers often choose FHA intentionally. They understand that preserving cash, maintaining liquidity, and entering the market earlier can create stronger long-term outcomes. FHA loans allow borrowers to keep reserves for emergencies, investments, or future opportunities rather than tying up every dollar in a down payment. This mindset separates reactive borrowers from strategic ones. FHA does not reward perfection; it rewards preparation and understanding. One of the most dangerous myths is the belief that borrowers must wait until their credit is flawless. FHA guidelines allow for lower credit scores, past credit events, and alternative compensating factors. Late payments, collections, and even previous bankruptcies do not automatically disqualify a borrower. What matters most is recovery, stability, and current behavior. Many borrowers delay homeownership unnecessarily, not realizing that they already meet FHA standards or could meet them with minimal adjustments. This delay often costs far more than improving credit while already owning a home.

Another misunderstanding involves income requirements. Many borrowers assume FHA requires traditional W-2 income only. In truth, FHA guidelines accommodate self-employed borrowers, gig workers, commission earners, and those with multiple income sources. While documentation is required, the program itself is far more flexible than commonly believed. Borrowers often disqualify themselves mentally before ever speaking with a knowledgeable lender. This self-elimination is one of the most common—and costly—mistakes in the FHA process.

There is also the myth that FHA loans lock borrowers into a bad loan forever. FHA loans are not permanent commitments;

they are tools. Borrowers can refinance, restructure, or transition into other loan types when their financial profile improves. FHA streamline refinances, rate-and-term refinances, and cash-out options provide flexibility that many borrowers never explore. Smart borrowers view FHA as a starting point, not a final destination. They understand that the first loan does not have to be the last loan.

Perhaps the most overlooked myth is that timing the market is safer than entering it. Many borrowers wait for lower rates, lower prices, or “better conditions.” Meanwhile, rents rise, home prices increase, and opportunity costs accumulate. FHA loans were designed to help borrowers move forward responsibly, even in imperfect conditions. Waiting for the perfect moment often results in missing the best moment. FHA rewards borrowers who act with knowledge rather than fear.

At its core, the FHA myth trap exists because most people learn about mortgages through opinions instead of facts. FHA guidelines are written, public, and structured, yet few borrowers are taught how to interpret them. This chapter serves as a reset. FHA loans are not shortcuts, handouts, or traps—they are structured pathways. Borrowers who understand the rules gain leverage. Borrowers who rely on myths give it away.

As this book continues, you will learn how myths translate into real financial mistakes, and how informed borrowers avoid them. FHA loans do not favor reckless decisions; they favor informed ones. The difference between winning and waiting is not income or credit—it is understanding. FHA loans reward borrowers who replace fear with facts and hesitation with strategy. This chapter is your first step out of the myth trap and into control of your homeownership journey.

The $38,000 Mistake: A Simple FHA Math Lesson

Maria and Daniel both earned $72,000 per year and rented similar apartments for $1,800 per month. Both wanted to buy a home, and both were told they should "wait" until they had perfect credit and 20% down. Daniel listened. Maria did the math.

Maria learned that FHA required only 3.5% down. She found a $300,000 home. Her down payment was $10,500. With closing costs and seller credits, she brought $13,000 total to closing. Her FHA loan amount was $289,500. Her monthly payment, including mortgage insurance, was $2,050. That was $250 more than rent.

Daniel decided to wait two more years to save 20% down. Over those two years, he paid $1,800 per month in rent. That totaled $43,200. During that same time, home prices increased by just 5% per year. The same home Maria bought for $300,000 now cost approximately $331,000. Maria made 24 mortgage payments of $2,050, totaling $49,200. Of that amount, roughly $10,800 went toward principal reduction and equity growth. Her home value also increased to $331,000. Her equity was now approximately $41,500, calculated as value minus loan balance.

Daniel finally bought the same type of home for $331,000. His 20% down payment was $66,200. He brought more than five times the cash Maria brought to closing. Despite avoiding mortgage insurance, he entered the market later, at a higher price, after spending $43,200 on rent with zero equity to show for it.

The math was simple. Maria used FHA to buy earlier, preserve cash, and build equity. Daniel waited for perfection and paid for patience. Maria did not "win" because she earned more or had better credit. She won because she understood FHA strategy instead of FHA myths.

That is the power of informed borrowing—and that is why FHA loans, when used correctly, change outcomes.

Chapter 2

Approval Is Not the Finish Line: The Hidden Mistakes Borrowers Make After "Getting Approved"

For many borrowers, receiving a loan preapproval feels like crossing the finish line. The anxiety fades, the pressure lifts, and the assumption sets in that the hard part is over. In reality, preapproval is not the end of the process—it is the beginning of the most fragile stage of the FHA loan journey. More FHA loans fall apart after preapproval than before it, not because borrowers suddenly become unqualified, but because they misunderstand what approval actually means. Approval is conditional, dynamic, and dependent on borrower behavior from the moment it is issued until the loan funds. This chapter exists to expose the costly mistakes borrowers make after "getting approved" and to show how informed borrowers protect their loan, their timeline, and their financial future.

One of the most common post-approval mistakes is changing financial behavior without realizing the consequences. Borrowers assume that because they have already been approved, they can safely open new credit, finance furniture, buy a car, or shift money between accounts. FHA underwriting does not stop at preapproval. Lenders re-verify credit, income, assets, and employment multiple times before closing. A single new credit inquiry, balance increase, or unexplained deposit can trigger a reassessment of the entire file. Borrowers who do not understand this process often sabotage their own loan without ever intending to.

Another major mistake occurs when borrowers misunderstand debt-to-income ratios. FHA allows higher ratios than many conventional programs, but that flexibility has limits. Borrowers often push those limits unknowingly by adding monthly obligations after approval. Even small payments—such as a $150 furniture payment or a $200 personal loan—can tip a loan from approvable to suspended. FHA underwriting evaluates ratios based on the full financial picture, not just gross income. Borrowers who treat approval as permission rather than responsibility frequently discover this too late.

Asset mismanagement is another silent loan killer. FHA allows gift funds, seller credits, and flexible asset sourcing, but documentation rules still apply. Borrowers sometimes move money between accounts, accept undocumented cash gifts, or deposit large sums without explanation. While the borrower may know exactly where the money came from, the lender must prove it. Unseasoned funds or unverifiable deposits can delay or derail a loan entirely. Smart borrowers understand that clarity matters more than convenience during the approval period.

Employment changes also pose a significant risk. FHA loans require income stability, not necessarily job permanence, but changes must be evaluated. Borrowers who switch jobs, change pay structure, reduce hours, or move from W-2 to self-employment after approval may unknowingly trigger a full income reassessment. Even positive changes—such as higher pay—can cause delays if documentation cannot be verified quickly. Borrowers often assume that better income automatically helps, when in reality, timing and documentation matter more than amount.

Another overlooked mistake involves property selection. FHA approval applies to the borrower, but the property must also meet FHA standards. Borrowers sometimes fall in love with homes that do not qualify—such as properties with safety issues, unpermitted additions, or HOA restrictions—without realizing the implications. Choosing the wrong property can result in appraisal conditions, repair requirements, or outright denial. Informed borrowers align their property search with FHA guidelines from the start, avoiding wasted time and emotional frustration. Communication breakdowns also contribute to post-approval problems. Borrowers sometimes delay responding to lender requests, underestimate the importance of documentation, or assume certain items are optional. FHA underwriting is detail-driven, and silence or delay creates risk. Borrowers who stay proactive, organized, and responsive move through the process smoothly. Those who disengage after approval often find themselves scrambling as deadlines approach.

Another major mistake is failing to plan for closing costs and cash-to-close changes. FHA loans allow seller contributions, but those contributions depend on contract terms, appraised value, and lender limits. Borrowers who assume their cash requirement is fixed may be surprised when adjustments occur. Smart borrowers maintain reserves, plan conservatively, and understand that final numbers can change slightly as the loan is finalized. This mindset prevents panic and last-minute funding issues.

Perhaps the most damaging mistake is emotional decision-making. Borrowers become impatient, frustrated, or overwhelmed and make rushed choices that affect their loan. They pressure sellers unnecessarily, ignore lender advice, or attempt to "fix" issues on their own. FHA loans reward calm, informed decision-making. Borrowers who understand the process treat approval as a partnership, not a guarantee. Approval is not a finish line—it is a responsibility. FHA loans offer flexibility, but that flexibility depends on borrower discipline. The most successful FHA borrowers are not those with the highest income or credit scores, but those who understand the rules and respect the process. This chapter serves as a reminder that winning with FHA is not about crossing one checkpoint; it is about protecting the entire path to closing.

How a $220 Payment Almost Cost $12,000

Jason was approved for an FHA loan at $280,000 with a 3.5% down payment. His lender calculated his debt-to-income ratio at 46%, safely within FHA limits. His estimated cash to close was $11,500 after seller credits, and his closing date was set for 30 days out. Jason felt relieved. In his mind, the hardest part was over.

Two weeks later, Jason decided to finance a living room set. The monthly payment was $220. He assumed it would not matter because his income was strong and the loan was already approved. When the lender pulled a final credit report before closing, the new account appeared.

The lender recalculated Jason's ratios. That $220 payment increased his debt-to-income ratio from 46% to 52%. FHA guidelines allowed the higher ratio only with additional compensating factors, which Jason's file did not have. The loan was suspended.

To fix the issue, Jason had two options. He could pay off the furniture loan entirely, or he could bring additional money to closing to reduce the loan amount. Paying off the furniture required $4,800 upfront. Reducing the loan required an additional $7,200 at closing to lower the monthly payment enough to offset the new debt.

Jason chose to bring cash. His original cash to close was $11,500. After the adjustment, it increased to $18,700. The $220 payment did not just cost him $220—it nearly cost him $12,000.

The loan closed, but barely. Jason learned that FHA approval is not static. Every financial decision during the loan process carries weight. The math was simple, but the lesson was expensive.

Borrowers who understand FHA strategy protect their approval. Borrowers who assume approval is permanent pay for that assumption.

Chapter 3

The Credit Illusion: Why "Good Enough" Credit Still Gets FHA Borrowers Denied

Credit is one of the most misunderstood parts of the FHA loan process. Many borrowers believe that once their credit score reaches a certain number, approval becomes automatic. Others assume that because FHA allows lower scores, credit quality no longer matters. Both assumptions are wrong. FHA underwriting does not rely on credit scores alone; it evaluates patterns, timing, behavior, and risk signals that numbers by themselves cannot capture. This chapter exists to dismantle the illusion that "good enough" credit is sufficient and to explain why some borrowers with higher scores are denied while others with lower scores are approved.

The first mistake borrowers make is focusing on the score rather than the story behind it. FHA underwriters look closely at recent payment history, especially within the last twelve months. A borrower with a 640 score and clean recent history may be viewed more favorably than a borrower with a 700 score who has recent late payments. FHA is designed to reward recovery, not perfection. Borrowers who improve their habits and demonstrate stability often qualify faster than those who rely on old achievements. The score is a snapshot; the behavior is the narrative.

Another critical misunderstanding involves collections and charge-offs. Many borrowers believe that all collections must be paid before closing, while others believe they can ignore them completely. FHA treats collections differently depending on the type, amount, and timing. Medical collections are generally excluded from debt calculations, while non-medical collections may require a hypothetical payment. Borrowers who fail to understand this distinction often make unnecessary payments that lower their cash reserves or, worse, activate old accounts and reduce their credit score right before closing. Knowledge—not action alone—is what protects borrowers here.

Credit utilization is another silent factor that trips up FHA borrowers. Many applicants carry revolving balances that are technically acceptable but strategically harmful. FHA underwriting considers the minimum monthly payments associated with credit cards, not the balances themselves. Borrowers who keep balances high, even temporarily, inflate their debt-to-income ratios and weaken their approval profile. Paying down balances at the wrong time, however, can also cause issues if it results in large, unexplained withdrawals.

Smart borrowers manage utilization deliberately and with guidance rather than making emotional credit decisions.

The timing of credit activity is equally important. Borrowers often attempt to "fix" their credit too close to application or closing. Opening new accounts, disputing accounts incorrectly, or engaging in rapid credit repair strategies can backfire. FHA requires disputes on derogatory accounts to be resolved before underwriting, which can delay or suspend approval. Additionally, newly opened accounts—even with zero balances—can lower average account age and trigger underwriting questions. Credit improvement is a process, not a last-minute rescue.

Authorized user accounts also create confusion. While authorized user accounts can help credit scores, FHA lenders evaluate whether the borrower is truly responsible for the debt. If payments are late or balances are high, the authorized account may harm more than help. Borrowers who rely on authorized user strategies without understanding lender overlays often discover that the account is excluded from consideration or becomes a liability rather than a benefit.

One of the most damaging credit mistakes FHA borrowers make is ignoring the importance of cash reserves as a compensating factor. FHA allows higher risk tolerance when borrowers demonstrate financial stability through savings. Borrowers who deplete reserves to pay off small debts or collections may weaken their overall file, even if their credit score improves slightly. FHA underwriting is about balance. A borrower with modest credit but strong reserves often presents less risk than one with higher scores and no savings.

Another common error involves credit inquiries. Borrowers often shop for credit products during the loan process, assuming that inquiries no longer matter once they are approved. FHA lenders must evaluate all inquiries within a specific timeframe, and unexplained inquiries can delay closing or require additional documentation. Each inquiry signals potential new debt, even if no account is opened. Borrowers who understand this avoid unnecessary credit activity until after closing.

The most important concept in FHA credit evaluation is intent. Underwriters look for signs of responsibility, recovery, and sustainability. Credit behavior tells a story about how a borrower handles obligations under stress, change, and opportunity. FHA loans are not designed for borrowers who chase short-term fixes; they are designed for those who demonstrate long-term stability. This is why some borrowers with "good" credit are denied while others with imperfect profiles are approved. Understanding FHA credit guidelines transforms credit from an obstacle into a tool. Borrowers who stop chasing numbers and start managing behavior gain control over their approval outcomes. FHA does not punish past mistakes; it evaluates present discipline. This chapter is not about achieving perfect credit—it is about avoiding unnecessary mistakes and presenting a profile that aligns with FHA's purpose. When borrowers understand the credit illusion, they stop reacting and start planning.

How a 702 Credit Score Failed and a 618 Score Closed

Kevin had a 702 credit score. Angela had a 618. On paper, Kevin appeared to be the stronger borrower. Both applied for FHA loans within the same month, for similar purchase prices, and with similar incomes. Only one loan closed on time.

Kevin carried $18,000 in credit card balances spread across five cards. His minimum monthly payments totaled $540. Angela carried $3,200 in balances, with total minimum payments of $95. Kevin had paid one account late two months before applying. Angela had no late payments in the past eighteen months.

Kevin assumed his score protected him. He decided to pay off two cards just before underwriting, withdrawing $6,000 from savings. His score increased slightly, but his reserves dropped below the lender's comfort threshold. The underwriter flagged the withdrawals and required documentation Kevin could not immediately provide.

Angela followed her lender's guidance. She paid down balances gradually three months before applying, keeping her reserves intact. Her debt-to-income ratio remained stable, and her file showed consistent behavior.

Kevin's FHA loan was suspended pending additional documentation and a re-evaluation of compensating factors. Angela's loan moved to clear-to-close without conditions.

The math explained the outcome. Kevin's $540 in monthly credit payments increased his debt-to-income ratio by over 6%. Angela's $95 increased hers by less than 1%. Kevin reduced reserves to chase points. Angela preserved stability.

Kevin's score looked better. Angela's profile performed better.

FHA did not choose the higher number. It chose the stronger story.

Chapter 4

The Wrong Guide Costs the Most: How Choosing the Wrong Lender Derails FHA Borrowers

Most FHA borrowers believe their biggest risk is credit, income, or down payment. In reality, one of the most expensive and least discussed mistakes borrowers make is choosing the wrong lender. FHA loans are governed by federal guidelines, but they are executed by private lenders—and those lenders vary widely in experience, interpretation, overlays, and borrower support. Two borrowers with identical financial profiles can receive completely different outcomes depending on who originates their loan. This chapter exposes how lender choice quietly determines approval success, cost, stress level, and long-term results.

One of the most misunderstood aspects of FHA lending is lender overlays. While FHA publishes baseline guidelines, individual lenders are allowed to impose stricter rules. These overlays can include higher minimum credit scores, lower debt-to-income limits, additional reserve requirements, or restrictions on certain property types. Borrowers are rarely told when a denial is caused by an overlay rather than FHA itself. As a result, many borrowers assume they are unqualified when, in reality, they simply chose a lender whose rules were unnecessarily restrictive.

Another common mistake is assuming all lenders price FHA loans the same. Interest rates, mortgage insurance handling, lender credits, and fees vary widely. Some lenders advertise low rates but charge high fees. Others offer higher rates with lender credits that reduce cash to close. Borrowers who focus only on rate without understanding total loan cost often pay thousands more over time. FHA loans require strategic pricing analysis, not headline comparison.

Communication style also matters more than borrowers expect. FHA loans involve documentation, explanations, and timing. Lenders who are slow to respond, vague in their guidance, or reactive rather than proactive increase borrower risk. Borrowers often blame themselves for delays or issues that originate from poor lender communication. A knowledgeable FHA lender anticipates problems before they occur and guides borrowers through them calmly and clearly.

Another overlooked issue is FHA specialization. Many lenders claim to “do FHA,” but only a subset handle FHA loans consistently and efficiently. FHA underwriting has nuances that differ from conventional loans, especially regarding credit history, self-employment, collections, and property standards. Lenders who rarely originate FHA loans may misinterpret guidelines, over-condition files, or escalate minor issues unnecessarily. Borrowers pay the price for this in delays, stress, and sometimes denial.

The preapproval process itself can be misleading. Some lenders issue quick approvals without fully reviewing documents, income, or credit details. These superficial approvals give borrowers false confidence and lead to problems later in underwriting. A thorough FHA preapproval may take more time upfront, but it prevents surprises during escrow. Borrowers who choose speed over substance often regret it.

Another costly mistake involves lender selection based solely on relationships. Borrowers may choose a lender recommended by a friend, family member, or real estate agent without verifying FHA expertise. While referrals can be valuable, FHA loans require specific competence. Loyalty does not replace qualification. Borrowers must treat lender selection as a strategic decision, not a courtesy.

The lender's role extends beyond closing. FHA loans offer refinance options, mortgage insurance considerations, and long-term planning opportunities. Lenders who fail to educate borrowers on future strategies leave them unprepared to leverage FHA benefits fully. Smart borrowers choose lenders who think beyond the transaction and understand the borrower's long-term goals.

Choosing the wrong lender does not just increase cost—it increases risk. Borrowers lose leverage, miss opportunities, and sometimes lose homes due to delays or missteps. FHA loans are forgiving programs, but they still require precision. The lender is the interpreter of the rules, the manager of the process, and the advocate for the borrower. When that role is poorly executed, the borrower pays for it.

This chapter is not about blaming lenders; it is about borrower awareness. FHA loans work best when borrowers partner with lenders who understand the program deeply and communicate transparently. The difference between a smooth closing and a collapsed deal is often not the borrower's qualifications, but the guide they chose to navigate the process.

The Same Borrower, Two Lenders, a $21,400 Difference

Elena applied for an FHA loan to purchase a $325,000 home. Her credit score was 636, her income was $82,000 per year, and she had $14,000 saved. She first applied with a large national lender that advertised low FHA rates. The lender required a minimum 660 credit score due to internal overlays.

Elena was denied and told she needed six months of credit improvement. She continued renting at $2,000 per month.

Three months later, Elena spoke with an FHA-specialized lender. That lender followed FHA baseline guidelines, not overlays. Elena was approved immediately with a 3.5% down payment of $11,375. Her cash to close after credits was $13,200.

Her FHA payment was $2,250 per month. That was $250 more than rent. Over the next twelve months, Elena paid $27,000 in mortgage payments. Of that amount, approximately $6,800 went toward principal reduction and equity. The home appreciated modestly by 4%, increasing its value to $338,000.

Had Elena waited the six months recommended by the first lender, she would have paid $12,000 more in rent. The home price would have increased to approximately $335,000. Her down payment requirement would have risen by $350. Her total cash to close would have increased, not decreased.

Additionally, the first lender's rate was 0.375% higher than the second lender's actual locked rate once fees were considered. Over five years, that rate difference would have cost Elena approximately $8,700 in additional interest.

The math was clear. One lender's overlay cost Elena time, rent, and opportunity. The right lender saved her over $21,400 in the first year alone.

Same borrower. Same FHA program. Completely different outcome.

Chapter 5

When the House Fails the Loan: FHA Property Rules That Borrowers Ignore Until It's Too Late

Many FHA borrowers believe that once they are approved, the rest of the process is simply paperwork and waiting. What they often discover—sometimes painfully late—is that FHA loans approve both the borrower and the property. A borrower can be fully qualified on paper and still lose the deal because the home does not meet FHA standards. This chapter exists to expose one of the most underestimated risks in FHA lending: choosing a property that quietly violates FHA guidelines and triggers appraisal conditions, repair demands, delays, or outright denial.

FHA property standards are not cosmetic preferences; they are safety, habitability, and livability requirements. The program was designed to protect borrowers from purchasing homes with hidden hazards or structural problems that could become financial burdens. However, many borrowers misunderstand these rules and assume that FHA standards apply only to extreme cases. In reality, relatively common property issues—such as peeling paint, missing handrails, roof wear, electrical concerns, or water intrusion—can create significant obstacles. Borrowers who fail to understand this often fall in love with homes that are incompatible with FHA financing.

One of the most common FHA property mistakes involves deferred maintenance. FHA does not require a home to be perfect, but it does require it to be safe and functional. Small issues, when combined, can signal neglect to an FHA appraiser. Borrowers often underestimate how minor defects accumulate into a larger problem. What appears manageable to a buyer may be unacceptable to an appraiser tasked with enforcing FHA standards. This disconnect leads to surprise repair requirements that derail timelines and negotiations.

Another major misunderstanding involves appraisal conditions. FHA appraisals are not simply valuations; they are inspections for minimum property standards. Borrowers often assume that if a home appraises at value, it automatically qualifies. In reality, the appraiser may assign conditions that must be resolved before closing. These conditions can include repairs that sellers are unwilling or unable to complete. Borrowers who do not plan for this possibility often lose leverage late in the process.

Condos and townhomes present additional complexity. FHA approval requires that the condominium project itself meet

FHA eligibility requirements. Many borrowers do not realize that individual units cannot be financed with FHA if the project is not approved. Buyers discover this only after making offers, paying inspection fees, or entering escrow. This mistake is particularly costly because it is entirely preventable with early verification.

Fixer-upper properties create another layer of risk. FHA does allow renovation loans, but standard FHA purchase loans do not permit significant repairs after closing. Borrowers sometimes assume they can handle repairs themselves later, only to learn that FHA requires issues to be addressed before funding. Without proper planning, borrowers may be forced to renegotiate contracts, switch loan programs, or walk away entirely.

Another overlooked factor is seller cooperation. FHA loans often require seller participation for repairs or credits. Sellers unfamiliar with FHA may resist these requirements, viewing them as burdensome. Borrowers who choose FHA without considering seller flexibility sometimes find themselves in conflict late in the transaction. In competitive markets, this can be particularly challenging if sellers prefer conventional buyers to avoid perceived complications. Timing is also critical. FHA repair requirements can extend closing timelines. Borrowers who are working with tight deadlines, lease expirations, or rate locks may find themselves under pressure if repairs take longer than expected. Smart borrowers build buffer time into their contracts and understand that FHA appraisals require patience and planning.

Perhaps the most damaging mistake borrowers make is assuming that property issues are personal failures rather than procedural realities. FHA guidelines are not judgments; they are safeguards. Borrowers who understand this approach property selection differently. They view the home through the lens of compliance, not emotion. This mindset dramatically increases success rates and reduces stress.

Choosing the right property is as important as choosing the right lender. FHA borrowers who understand property standards upfront avoid heartbreak, wasted money, and lost opportunities. This chapter is not meant to discourage FHA buyers from purchasing homes—it is meant to empower them to choose wisely. When borrowers align their property choice with FHA guidelines, the process becomes predictable rather than chaotic.

FHA loans do not fail randomly. They fail at predictable friction points that informed borrowers can anticipate and manage. Property compliance is one of those points. Borrowers who respect FHA property rules gain control over their timeline, negotiation power, and closing outcome. Those who ignore them learn the lesson the hard way.

The $9,600 Repair Surprise That Almost Killed the Deal

Tanya was approved for an FHA loan to purchase a $295,000 home. Her down payment was $10,325, and her estimated cash to close was $12,400 after seller credits. The home looked perfect to her—new paint, updated kitchen, and a large backyard. She assumed the appraisal would be routine.

The FHA appraisal came back at value, but with conditions. The appraiser noted peeling paint on exterior trim, a missing handrail on the back steps, a roof with less than two years of remaining life, and an electrical outlet near the sink that was not GFCI protected. Individually, these issues seemed minor. Collectively, they triggered mandatory repairs.

Contractors estimated the total cost of repairs at $9,600. FHA required the repairs to be completed before closing. The seller refused to pay, stating that the home had already passed inspection for previous buyers. Tanya was given three options: renegotiate, switch loan programs, or cancel the contract.

Switching to a conventional loan required a 5% down payment instead of 3.5%, increasing Tanya's down payment by $4,425. Her interest rate would also be higher, increasing her monthly payment by $185. Over five years, that rate difference would cost approximately $11,100 in additional interest.

Renegotiating meant asking the seller to reduce the price by $9,600 so Tanya could finance repairs later. The seller countered with a $4,000 reduction. Tanya would still need to bring $5,600 more to closing.

After reviewing the math, Tanya chose to walk away. She lost $1,200 in inspections and appraisal fees but avoided a long-term financial setback. Two weeks later, she found a different FHA-compliant home for $290,000 with no repair conditions.

The lesson was clear. The first home did not fail because Tanya was unqualified. It failed because the property did not meet FHA standards. The $9,600 surprise was not random—it was predictable.

In FHA lending, the house must qualify just as much as the borrower. Understanding that distinction saved Tanya from a costly mistake.

Chapter 6

The Mortgage Insurance Myth: Why FHA MIP Isn't the Enemy—and How Smart Borrowers Escape It

Few elements of FHA loans generate as much fear and confusion as mortgage insurance. Borrowers hear phrases like "FHA mortgage insurance lasts forever" or "FHA loans are too expensive because of MIP," and many immediately disqualify the program without ever running the numbers. Mortgage insurance becomes the villain in the story, blamed for keeping borrowers stuck or making FHA loans inferior. In reality, mortgage insurance is neither good nor bad on its own—it is a tool. Like any tool, its value depends on how it is used, how long it is used, and whether the borrower understands the exit strategy from the beginning.

FHA mortgage insurance exists to protect lenders, not punish borrowers. By insuring the loan, FHA allows lenders to offer lower down payments, more flexible credit standards, and higher debt-to-income ratios. Without mortgage insurance, most FHA borrowers would not qualify at all. The mistake borrowers make is evaluating mortgage insurance in isolation instead of comparing it to the cost of waiting, renting, or bringing significantly more cash to closing. Mortgage insurance is not the cost of failure—it is the cost of access.

One of the most common myths is that FHA mortgage insurance lasts forever. While it is true that many FHA loans issued today require mortgage insurance for the life of the loan, this does not mean the borrower is trapped. FHA loans were never intended to remain unchanged for 30 years. They are designed to be refinanced, restructured, or transitioned when the borrower's financial profile improves. Smart borrowers do not ask, "How long does MIP last?" They ask, "How long do I plan to keep this loan?"

Another misunderstanding involves the upfront mortgage insurance premium. FHA charges an upfront premium that is often financed into the loan. Borrowers see this as an unnecessary cost without recognizing its purpose. That upfront premium allows FHA to offer more forgiving approval standards across millions of borrowers. When spread over time and compared to the benefits gained—earlier ownership, lower down payment, preserved cash—the cost becomes far less intimidating. The problem is not the premium; the problem is the lack of context.

Monthly mortgage insurance is also misunderstood. Borrowers often fixate on the monthly MIP amount without comparing it to rent increases, lost equity, or the opportunity cost of delaying ownership. A borrower paying $140 per month in MIP may build $10,000 to $20,000 in equity during the same period. When viewed in isolation, MIP looks expensive. When viewed in context, it often looks strategic.

Another critical mistake borrowers make is failing to plan their MIP exit before closing. FHA borrowers who enter the loan without a refinance or equity strategy feel trapped later. Borrowers who plan ahead understand that mortgage insurance is temporary by design, even if it is technically permanent on paper. Rising property values, principal reduction, income growth, and credit improvement all create exit opportunities. FHA rewards borrowers who think in phases rather than lifetimes.

Timing plays a major role in mortgage insurance strategy. Refinancing too early may not reduce costs enough to justify the transaction. Refinancing too late may result in years of unnecessary payments. Borrowers who track their loan balance, market conditions, and credit profile can identify optimal refinance windows. FHA streamline refinances, conventional refinances, and even FHA-to-FHA transitions can all play a role depending on the borrower's situation. Another myth is that conventional loans automatically eliminate mortgage insurance. Many conventional borrowers pay private mortgage insurance for years, often at higher effective costs than FHA MIP. Additionally, conventional loans often require higher credit scores and stricter ratios, which may delay entry into the market. FHA mortgage insurance is transparent, standardized, and predictable—qualities that can work in the borrower's favor.

The emotional reaction to mortgage insurance often causes borrowers to make poor decisions. Some overextend themselves to avoid MIP, draining savings or taking on riskier loan terms. Others wait years to save larger down payments while paying rising rents. Mortgage insurance becomes the excuse rather than the issue. Smart borrowers separate emotion from math.

Mortgage insurance should be evaluated as part of a broader wealth strategy. FHA loans allow borrowers to buy sooner, preserve liquidity, and participate in appreciation. Those benefits often outweigh the cost of MIP by a wide margin. The key is not avoiding mortgage insurance—it is controlling how long you pay it.

This chapter is not an argument in favor of permanent FHA loans. It is an argument for informed borrowing. Mortgage insurance is not a life sentence; it is a bridge. Borrowers who understand that bridge cross it deliberately, exit it strategically, and use FHA loans as stepping stones rather than anchors. The real mistake is not paying mortgage insurance—it is paying it without a plan.

The $168 Monthly Fee That Built $52,000 in Wealth

Brian purchased a home using an FHA loan for $310,000 with a 3.5% down payment of $10,850. His loan amount, including the upfront mortgage insurance premium, was $304,700. His monthly mortgage insurance payment was $168. Brian initially hesitated, focusing on that monthly cost.

Over the first three years, Brian paid approximately $6,048 in monthly mortgage insurance. During that same period, his home appreciated at a modest average rate of 5% per year. After three years, the home's value increased to approximately $359,000.

Brian's loan balance after three years was approximately $291,000. His equity position was now roughly $68,000, calculated as market value minus loan balance. Even after accounting for the $6,048 in mortgage insurance payments, Brian had gained over $61,000 in net equity.

Had Brian waited three years to avoid mortgage insurance, he would have continued renting at $2,100 per month. Over three years, that rent totaled $75,600 with no equity gained.

Additionally, the same home would have cost $359,000 instead of $310,000, increasing his down payment requirement and total loan amount.

At the three-year mark, Brian refinanced into a conventional loan. His improved credit score and lower loan-to-value ratio eliminated mortgage insurance entirely. His new payment dropped by $210 per month, even with a slightly higher interest rate.

The math was undeniable. The $168 monthly mortgage insurance payment was not a penalty—it was the price of early access. That access allowed Brian to capture appreciation, build equity, and exit the loan on his terms.

Mortgage insurance did not cost Brian money. It made him money—because he used it with a plan.

Chapter 7

The Timing Trap: How FHA Borrowers Miss Refinance Windows and Lose Years of Wealth

Timing is the invisible factor that determines whether an FHA loan becomes a stepping stone to wealth or a long-term drag on cash flow. Many borrowers believe refinancing is something to consider "someday," without realizing that refinance opportunities appear and disappear in specific windows. FHA borrowers who fail to recognize these windows often pay mortgage insurance longer than necessary, miss lower interest rates, or delay access to equity. This chapter exists to explain why timing—not just qualification—separates borrowers who win with FHA loans from those who simply get by.

One of the most common misconceptions is that refinancing should only be considered when interest rates drop significantly. While rates matter, they are only one piece of the equation. FHA refinance opportunities are influenced by loan seasoning, payment history, equity position, credit improvement, and market appreciation. Borrowers who wait for a perfect rate environment often miss the optimal moment when these factors align. FHA loans reward proactive monitoring, not passive waiting.

Another timing mistake involves misunderstanding seasoning requirements. FHA streamline refinances require a minimum number of on-time payments and a waiting period before eligibility. Borrowers who do not track these milestones may delay action unnecessarily. Conversely, borrowers who attempt to refinance too early may incur costs that outweigh the benefits. Timing is about balance. Refinancing is most powerful when the borrower has gained enough benefit from the original loan to justify the transition.

Equity growth is another misunderstood driver of refinance timing. Many FHA borrowers underestimate how quickly equity can accumulate through appreciation and principal reduction. Small monthly payments toward principal, combined with modest market growth, can create refinance opportunities sooner than expected. Borrowers who fail to track their loan-to-value ratio often miss the moment when they qualify for conventional financing and can eliminate mortgage insurance entirely.

Credit improvement also plays a critical role. FHA borrowers frequently improve their credit profiles after closing due to stabilized housing costs and reduced reliance on credit. Borrowers who assume their credit will always be "not quite ready" often delay refinancing far longer than necessary. In reality, many borrowers qualify for better terms within 12 to 24 months of consistent payments. Monitoring credit trends—not just scores—allows borrowers to act strategically.

Another costly timing error involves market cycles. Borrowers often react emotionally to headlines rather than evaluating their personal financial position. Rising rates may discourage refinancing even when mortgage insurance elimination or term restructuring still produces net savings. Falling rates may trigger panic refinancing without proper cost-benefit analysis. FHA borrowers who anchor decisions to personal math rather than market noise make better long-term choices.

The FHA streamline refinance is one of the most underutilized tools in the program. Designed to reduce payment and risk with minimal documentation, it allows borrowers to improve terms without a full credit or income re-verification in many cases. Borrowers who are unaware of this option miss opportunities to lower payments or prepare for later transitions into conventional loans.

Another timing mistake occurs when borrowers confuse loan duration with loan strategy. FHA loans are not meant to be held indefinitely in their original form. They are dynamic instruments that evolve with the borrower's financial life.

Borrowers who assume they must stay in the same loan structure for decades fail to leverage the flexibility FHA offers. Strategic borrowers treat their mortgage as an evolving asset, not a static obligation.

Perhaps the most damaging timing error is procrastination disguised as caution. Borrowers tell themselves they are "waiting for the right time" without defining what that means. Meanwhile, months turn into years, and small inefficiencies compound into large losses. FHA loans reward awareness. Borrowers who track their numbers, understand their options, and act decisively gain control over their financial timeline.

Timing is not about predicting the market—it is about recognizing readiness. FHA borrowers who understand their loan metrics, equity position, and financial trajectory do not wait for perfect conditions. They act when the math works. This chapter is a reminder that wealth is built not only by access to programs, but by the ability to act at the right moment.

The 14-Month Delay That Cost $31,800

Sophia purchased her home with an FHA loan for $285,000, putting down 3.5% or $9,975. Her loan amount after the upfront mortgage insurance premium was $279,800. Her monthly payment included $162 in mortgage insurance. At the time, she accepted this cost as part of the deal.

After 18 months of on-time payments, Sophia's credit score improved from 632 to 704. Her loan balance dropped to approximately $271,000. Meanwhile, her home appreciated at an average rate of 6% annually. The property was now worth approximately $320,000. Her loan-to-value ratio had fallen below 85%, qualifying her for a conventional refinance with no mortgage insurance.

Sophia's lender recommended refinancing immediately. The new payment would eliminate the $162 monthly mortgage insurance and reduce her interest rate slightly. The refinance costs were estimated at $5,200, which could be recouped in less than three years through monthly savings.

Sophia hesitated, believing rates might fall further. She waited 14 months. During that time, she paid an additional $2,268 in mortgage insurance. Rates increased by 0.75%. When she finally refinanced, her new rate was higher than it would have been earlier. Her monthly payment decreased by only $68 instead of the projected $210.

Over the 14-month delay, Sophia paid $2,268 in unnecessary mortgage insurance. Over the next five years, the higher interest rate cost her approximately $29,500 in additional interest compared to the earlier refinance option. The total cost of waiting was roughly $31,800.

The math told the story. The refinance window was open. Sophia saw it but did not act. FHA gave her the opportunity. Timing determined the outcome.

Borrowers who understand FHA timing do not wait for perfect conditions. They act when readiness and math align—and that decision changes everything.

Chapter 8

Equity Is Not Income: How FHA Cash-Out Mistakes Turn Opportunity into Debt

Home equity is one of the most powerful financial resources a homeowner can build, yet it is also one of the easiest to misuse. FHA cash-out refinances promise flexibility and access to capital, but they also carry risk when misunderstood or mistimed. Many borrowers treat equity like a paycheck rather than a strategic asset, assuming that if money is available, it should be used. This chapter exists to clarify the difference between leveraging equity intelligently and converting long-term wealth into short-term relief that creates lasting financial strain.

FHA cash-out refinances are designed to allow homeowners to access equity while maintaining reasonable underwriting standards. They can be used for debt consolidation, home improvements, investment, or major expenses. The mistake borrowers make is assuming that access equals affordability. Just because equity can be converted into cash does not mean the resulting loan structure supports long-term stability. FHA underwriting evaluates the new payment, not the borrower's intentions. Borrowers who fail to analyze post-refinance cash flow often discover too late that the transaction solved a short-term problem while creating a long-term one.

One of the most common cash-out mistakes is using equity to pay off consumer debt without changing spending behavior. FHA borrowers consolidate credit cards, personal loans, or auto balances into a new mortgage, celebrating the lower monthly payment. Without discipline, those same credit balances often return within months, leaving the borrower with higher mortgage debt and renewed unsecured obligations. Equity that took years to build disappears in a single transaction, replaced by habits that continue to erode financial health.

Another major error involves refinancing at the wrong point in the rate cycle. FHA cash-out refinances often come with higher interest rates than rate-and-term refinances. Borrowers who rush into cash-out transactions during rising rate environments may lock in long-term costs that far exceed the value of the cash received. Timing matters. A cash-out refinance should be evaluated not only by how much cash is received, but by how much additional interest will be paid over time.

Loan-to-value limits also play a critical role. FHA cash-out refinances typically cap the loan at a percentage of the home's value. Borrowers who extract equity aggressively reduce their buffer against market changes. A modest market correction can eliminate remaining equity entirely, trapping borrowers in high loan-to-value positions and limiting future refinance or sale options. Equity is a cushion. Removing too much of it increases vulnerability.

Another overlooked factor is mortgage insurance. FHA cash-out refinances reset mortgage insurance terms, often extending the duration of payments. Borrowers who previously planned to refinance out of FHA may unknowingly restart the clock, paying mortgage insurance far longer than expected. This mistake is especially costly for borrowers who could have transitioned to conventional financing with proper planning.

The purpose of the cash-out also matters. Using equity to improve the property can increase value and offset the cost of borrowing. Using equity for depreciating expenses—such as vacations, vehicles, or lifestyle upgrades—rarely produces a return. FHA does not restrict how cash-out funds are used, but borrowers must restrict themselves. Equity should be treated as invested capital, not disposable income.

Another mistake involves ignoring tax and opportunity costs. Mortgage interest may be deductible for some borrowers, but that does not make it free. Borrowers who compare cash-out proceeds only to monthly payment changes often miss the long-term cost of interest paid over decades. A $40,000 cash-out may cost $90,000 or more over the life of the loan. Without a clear return on that capital, the transaction becomes a wealth transfer from borrower to lender.

Emotional decision-making also drives poor cash-out outcomes. Borrowers refinance under stress—job loss, medical expenses, or urgent financial pressure—without evaluating alternatives. While FHA cash-out refinances can provide relief in emergencies, they should be structured carefully and viewed as temporary solutions. Permanent changes should not be made under temporary pressure.

The most successful FHA borrowers approach cash-out refinances with the same discipline they apply to investments. They evaluate return, risk, timing, and exit strategy. They ask whether the transaction improves their balance sheet, not just their bank balance. FHA cash-out refinances can be powerful wealth tools when used intentionally, but they can also be silent wealth destroyers when used impulsively.

Equity is not income. It is stored value. FHA gives borrowers access to that value, but it does not protect them from misuse. This chapter is not a warning against cash-out refinances—it is a reminder that leverage amplifies decisions. Used wisely, equity accelerates progress. Used poorly, it delays it for years.

The $45,000 Cash-Out That Cost $112,000

Marcus purchased his home five years ago for $260,000 using an FHA loan. Over time, the property appreciated to $335,000, and his loan balance dropped to approximately $235,000. He now had roughly $100,000 in equity. Feeling financially stretched, Marcus decided to take an FHA cash-out refinance.

Marcus refinanced into a new FHA loan for $280,000, pulling out $45,000 in cash after fees. His new interest rate was 1% higher than his previous rate, and his mortgage insurance clock reset. His monthly payment increased by $290, but his credit card payments disappeared. The relief felt immediate.

Over the next three years, Marcus rebuilt $28,000 in credit card debt. His mortgage balance declined slowly due to the higher interest rate. When he reviewed his numbers, he discovered that the $45,000 cash-out would cost approximately $112,000 in total interest over the life of the loan.

Had Marcus instead used a portion of his savings and a structured debt payoff plan, he could have avoided refinancing entirely. Alternatively, a smaller cash-out combined with spending changes would have preserved equity and reduced long-term costs. The math was unforgiving. The $45,000 he accessed solved a short-term problem but created a long-term obligation that more than doubled the cost of the original cash received.

Equity did not fail Marcus. Misunderstanding it did.

Chapter 9

House Hacking Gone Wrong: The FHA Multi-Unit Mistakes That Cap Wealth Instead of Creating It

Few FHA strategies are as powerful—or as misunderstood—as buying a multi-unit property and living in one unit while renting the others. Often called "house hacking," this approach allows borrowers to use FHA's low down payment to acquire income-producing real estate with minimal cash. When done correctly, it can accelerate wealth, reduce living expenses, and create long-term financial stability. When done poorly, it can trap borrowers in negative cash flow, underwriting stress, and missed opportunity. This chapter exists to separate the strategy from the hype and explain why many FHA multi-unit buyers fail to realize the full potential of this approach.

One of the most common mistakes FHA multi-unit borrowers make is misunderstanding how rental income is calculated. FHA does not allow borrowers to count all projected rent. Instead, lenders apply vacancy factors, operating assumptions, and documentation requirements. Borrowers who assume full rent will offset their mortgage often discover during underwriting that only a portion is usable. This miscalculation leads to higher debt-to-income ratios than expected and, in some cases, loan denial. FHA rewards conservative assumptions, not optimistic projections.

Another frequent error is underestimating operating costs. New multi-unit buyers often focus on gross rent without accounting for maintenance, utilities, property management, and reserves. FHA does not require formal operating statements for owner-occupied properties, but lenders still evaluate the borrower's ability to carry the full payment if rental income fluctuates. Borrowers who rely on every dollar of rent to survive place themselves in fragile financial positions. Cash flow must be resilient, not just positive on paper.

Property condition plays an even larger role in multi-unit FHA purchases. Multiple units mean multiple systems, tenants, and points of failure. FHA appraisal standards apply to every unit, not just the one the borrower occupies. Deferred maintenance in any unit can trigger repair requirements that delay closing or increase costs. Borrowers who underestimate this complexity often encounter surprises that strain budgets and timelines.

Tenant assumptions also create problems. Borrowers sometimes assume existing tenants will remain, pay on time, and cooperate with the transition. FHA underwriting does not guarantee tenant stability. Vacancies, turnover, and non-payment are realities of rental ownership. Borrowers who do not plan for these risks may find themselves covering full mortgage payments unexpectedly. FHA multi-unit success depends on buffers, not best-case scenarios.

Another mistake involves choosing the wrong unit mix. Two- to four-unit properties vary widely in cash flow potential. Borrowers who select properties based solely on purchase price may miss better opportunities with higher rental yield or lower maintenance burden. FHA allows up to four units, but more units do not automatically mean better results. Strategic selection matters more than scale.

Many borrowers also fail to consider long-term exit strategy. FHA multi-unit loans are powerful entry tools, but they should align with future goals. Borrowers who plan to move out and convert the property to full rental status must consider refinancing options, loan seasoning, and future financing constraints. Without a clear plan, borrowers may find themselves unable to leverage equity or expand their portfolio as expected.

Another overlooked factor is emotional tolerance. Living next to tenants requires patience, communication, and boundaries. Borrowers who are unprepared for this dynamic may experience stress that outweighs financial benefits. FHA does not account for lifestyle compatibility, but borrowers must.

The most successful FHA multi-unit borrowers approach the purchase as both homeowners and investors. They analyze numbers conservatively, plan for variability, and maintain reserves. They understand that the goal is not free housing—it is sustainable progress. FHA provides the access, but discipline determines the outcome.

House hacking is not a shortcut; it is a structured strategy. When borrowers ignore the details, the strategy fails. When they respect the math and the responsibility, FHA multi-unit properties become one of the fastest and safest ways to build wealth.

The Duplex That Looked Free—but Wasn't

Carlos purchased a duplex using an FHA loan for $420,000. He put down 3.5%, or $14,700. The appraiser estimated market rent of $1,800 per unit. Carlos planned to live in one unit and rent the other, expecting the rent to cover most of the mortgage.

The total monthly mortgage payment, including mortgage insurance, taxes, and insurance, was $3,150. Carlos assumed the $1,800 rent would reduce his out-of-pocket cost to $1,350.

FHA underwriting, however, allowed only 75% of projected rent to be counted, or $1,350. This reduced his qualifying offset by $450 per month.

After utilities and maintenance averaging $300 per month, Carlos's actual monthly cost was closer to $2,100. When the tenant moved out after eight months, Carlos covered the full payment for two months while re-renting. That added $6,300 in unexpected expenses.

Over the first year, Carlos spent $25,200 on housing, far more than the $16,200 he had projected. While the property appreciated modestly and built equity, the cash flow strain caused stress and delayed savings.

Had Carlos purchased a smaller duplex for $380,000 with stronger rental ratios, his payment would have been $2,750, and his usable rental income would have covered a larger portion of the mortgage. The math—not the concept—determined the outcome.

The duplex did not fail because FHA was flawed. It failed because assumptions replaced analysis.

House hacking works when numbers are conservative and buffers are real. FHA provides the leverage. The borrower must provide the discipline.

Chapter 10

The FHA Borrower's Playbook: How Smart Buyers Turn Rules into Long-Term Wealth

At this point in the series, one truth should be clear: FHA loans are not simple, but they are predictable. Every myth, mistake, delay, or financial setback explored in this book traces back to one underlying issue—borrowers either understand the rules and plan accordingly, or they react to the process without a strategy. FHA loans do not reward guesswork. They reward preparation, patience, and intentional decision-making. This final chapter exists to transform everything you have learned into a borrower mindset that lasts far beyond a single transaction.

Smart FHA borrowers do not see the loan as an isolated event. They see it as a phase in a longer financial journey. From the moment they apply, they think about cash flow, equity growth, refinance timing, and exit options. They understand that FHA is not designed to be "good" or "bad," but flexible. That flexibility becomes powerful only when paired with awareness. Borrowers who treat FHA loans as temporary stepping stones create options. Borrowers who treat them as permanent solutions often feel stuck.

The first rule in the FHA borrower's playbook is ownership of the process. Successful borrowers do not outsource responsibility entirely to lenders, agents, or online advice. They ask questions, verify assumptions, and track their own numbers. They understand their debt-to-income ratio, their loan-to-value position, and their credit trends. This awareness allows them to anticipate issues rather than react to them. FHA borrowers who remain passive are often surprised. Those who stay engaged remain in control.

Another defining characteristic of winning FHA borrowers is restraint. They do not rush into decisions simply because approval is granted or equity becomes available. They resist emotional choices—overpaying for homes, refinancing under pressure, or extracting equity without a plan. FHA loans provide access, but access without discipline leads to fragility. The strongest borrowers preserve liquidity, maintain reserves, and protect their margin of safety even when opportunities appear tempting.

Timing also separates successful borrowers from frustrated ones. FHA loans operate within clear timelines—seasoning periods, refinance windows, market cycles, and credit improvement phases. Borrowers who monitor these timelines position themselves to act decisively when opportunities arise. They do not wait indefinitely for perfection, nor do they jump at every change in rates or headlines. They act when readiness and math align. This balance turns FHA loans into momentum rather than drag.

Property selection is another cornerstone of the playbook. Smart borrowers do not choose homes based solely on aesthetics or emotion. They evaluate properties through the lens of FHA standards, long-term usability, and future flexibility. Whether purchasing a single-family home or a multi-unit property, they consider maintenance burden, resale potential, and compliance. They understand that a property that barely qualifies today may limit options tomorrow.

The FHA borrower's playbook also includes a clear mortgage insurance strategy. Winning borrowers do not fixate on the permanence of MIP; they plan its removal. They track appreciation, principal reduction, and credit improvement. They identify refinance triggers and revisit them regularly. Mortgage insurance becomes a known cost with a known exit—not an indefinite penalty. This shift in perspective changes how borrowers experience the loan emotionally and financially.

Another essential element is adaptability. Life changes. Income shifts, families grow, markets fluctuate. FHA borrowers who succeed long-term remain flexible. They understand that refinancing, restructuring, or selling are not failures—they are adjustments. FHA loans provide multiple paths forward, but only for borrowers willing to reassess and realign as circumstances evolve.

Perhaps the most important lesson in this entire series is that FHA loans do not create wealth by themselves. They create opportunity. Opportunity becomes wealth only when paired with informed decisions over time. Borrowers who use FHA loans to enter the market earlier, preserve cash, and build equity often outperform those who wait for ideal conditions. The compounding effect of ownership—appreciation, principal reduction, and stability—quietly outpaces fear-based hesitation.

This final chapter is not about mastering rules; it is about mastering mindset. FHA loans are forgiving, but they are not careless. They allow room for imperfection while rewarding consistency. Borrowers who understand this stop chasing approval and start designing outcomes. They stop fearing mistakes and start managing risk. They stop asking whether FHA is "worth it" and start asking how to use it best.

The FHA borrower's playbook is not complicated, but it is intentional. Know your numbers. Choose the right partners. Respect timing. Protect equity. Plan exits. Stay adaptable. When borrowers follow these principles, FHA loans become one of the most reliable wealth-building tools available to everyday buyers.

This book—and this series—ends here, but the strategy does not. FHA loans are not the finish line. They are the opening chapter of a longer story. How that story unfolds depends not on the program, but on the borrower who uses it.

From FHA to Freedom: The Eight-Year Blueprint That Worked

Lena purchased her first home using an FHA loan for $275,000 with a 3.5% down payment of $9,625. Her loan amount after upfront mortgage insurance was $270,800. Her monthly payment included $155 in mortgage insurance. At the time, she viewed FHA as her only option.

Over the first three years, Lena focused on stability. She made every payment on time, avoided new debt, and allowed her credit score to rise from 628 to 705. Her home appreciated modestly at 4% per year, reaching a value of approximately $310,000. Her loan balance dropped to $258,000.

At year three, Lena refinanced into a conventional loan. Mortgage insurance was eliminated. Her monthly payment dropped by $240. Instead of increasing her lifestyle, Lena redirected that savings into reserves.

Two years later, Lena purchased a duplex using another FHA loan, living in one unit and renting the other. The rental income offset most of her housing cost. Meanwhile, her original home continued appreciating.

By year eight, Lena owned two properties worth a combined $725,000. Her total mortgage balance was $465,000, giving her approximately $260,000 in equity. She had never earned a six-figure income, never used risky leverage, and never timed the market perfectly.

The math worked because the strategy was phased. FHA was not a shortcut—it was an entry point. Each decision built on the last.

Lena did not win because FHA was generous. She won because she understood how to use it.

That is the FHA borrower's playbook in action.

Chapter 11

The Silent Killers of FHA Success: Small Decisions That Quietly Destroy Big Outcomes

Most FHA borrowers do not fail dramatically. Their loans are not denied at the last minute, their closings do not collapse publicly, and their finances do not implode overnight. Instead, failure—when it happens—arrives quietly. It shows up in slightly higher payments, delayed refinances, drained reserves, missed opportunities, and years of lost momentum. These outcomes rarely stem from one large mistake. They are almost always the result of small, repeated decisions that seem harmless in isolation but compound over time. This chapter exists to expose those silent killers and show how disciplined borrowers avoid them.

One of the most dangerous silent killers is comfort. Once borrowers settle into their FHA loan, make payments on time, and adjust to homeownership, urgency fades. The loan becomes background noise rather than an active financial tool. Borrowers stop tracking loan balance, equity growth, or refinance eligibility. They assume stability equals optimization. In reality, complacency is expensive. FHA loans require periodic reassessment to remain efficient. Borrowers who stop paying attention almost always overpay longer than necessary.

Another silent killer is lifestyle drift. FHA borrowers often experience improved financial stability after buying a home. Rent is replaced with a fixed payment, credit improves, and confidence grows. Without discipline, spending rises to match that comfort. New cars, higher discretionary spending, and unnecessary debt creep in. These choices rarely cause immediate harm, but they quietly limit future refinancing options, increase debt ratios, and reduce flexibility. FHA borrowers who protect their upside understand that stability is an opportunity to strengthen—not expand—obligations.

A third silent killer is misunderstanding leverage. FHA loans are inherently leveraged products, allowing borrowers to control large assets with small down payments. Leverage magnifies outcomes—both positive and negative. Borrowers who treat leverage casually often extract equity too early, refinance unnecessarily, or chase short-term relief at long-term cost. FHA borrowers who succeed respect leverage as something to be earned repeatedly through performance, not something to be consumed all at once.

Another overlooked issue is the failure to define success. Many FHA borrowers enter the process with vague goals: "buy a home," "lower my payment," or "build wealth." Without specificity, decisions lack direction. Should equity be preserved or deployed? Should refinancing prioritize cash flow or speed? Should a move trigger a sale or a rental conversion? Borrowers who do not define success default to convenience—and convenience rarely aligns with optimal outcomes.

Time horizon confusion also undermines FHA success. Borrowers often mix short-term thinking with long-term commitments. They refinance thirty-year loans to solve twelve-month problems. They extract equity meant to compound over decades to address temporary discomfort. FHA loans are forgiving, but they are still long-term instruments. Borrowers who align loan decisions with realistic time horizons avoid regret. Those who do not often spend years undoing small, rushed choices.

Another silent killer is advisor dependency. Borrowers assume professionals will always act in their best interest. While many lenders and agents are ethical and competent, they are still transaction-focused by nature. The borrower is the only party responsible for long-term outcomes. FHA borrowers who outsource thinking lose leverage. Those who remain informed collaborators maintain control. Asking "why" is not distrust—it is strategy. Fear is another quiet saboteur. Borrowers fear refinancing mistakes, market shifts, or making the "wrong" move. That fear often masquerades as patience. Meanwhile, inefficiencies compound. FHA borrowers who succeed understand that inaction is still a decision—with measurable cost. They do not rush, but they do not freeze. They act when math supports movement, not when fear dissipates.

Perhaps the most subtle killer is identity. Some borrowers continue to see themselves as "lucky to be approved" long after they have proven reliability. This mindset leads to hesitation, over-accommodation, and under-assertion. FHA borrowers who build wealth eventually shift identity—from applicant to owner, from borrower to strategist. That shift changes behavior. Confidence grounded in numbers replaces insecurity grounded in myth.

This chapter is not about avoiding catastrophe. It is about avoiding erosion. FHA loans rarely fail loudly; they fail quietly through neglect, drift, and missed recalibration. Borrowers who win long-term treat their mortgage as a living system—reviewed, adjusted, and optimized periodically. They understand that wealth is not built by dramatic moves, but by consistent, disciplined alignment.

The silent killers only succeed when borrowers stop paying attention. Awareness is the antidote. FHA loans offer flexibility, but flexibility without vigilance becomes inefficiency. This final lesson reinforces a simple truth: success with FHA is not about doing everything right once—it is about avoiding small mistakes repeatedly over time.

The $19,000 Oversight That No One Warned Her About

Erica purchased her home using an FHA loan for $305,000 with a 3.5% down payment of $10,675. Her loan balance after upfront mortgage insurance was $300,400. Her mortgage insurance cost was $164 per month. At closing, Erica planned to “deal with refinancing later.”

After two years, Erica’s credit score improved from 641 to 712. Her loan balance dropped to approximately $292,000. Her home appreciated modestly to $340,000. Her loan-to-value ratio was now under 86%, making her eligible for a conventional refinance with no mortgage insurance.

Her lender mentioned refinancing casually, but Erica felt no urgency. Her payment felt manageable, and life was busy. She delayed.

Over the next 24 months, Erica paid an additional $3,936 in mortgage insurance. Interest rates rose by 0.875%. When she finally refinanced in year four, her new rate was higher than it would have been earlier. The higher rate increased her monthly payment by $118 compared to the earlier refinance scenario. Over five years, that difference totaled approximately $15,000 in additional interest. Combined with unnecessary mortgage insurance payments, Erica's delay cost her roughly $19,000.

No crisis occurred. No warning appeared. Nothing "went wrong." Erica simply failed to act during an optimal window.

The math was simple. The oversight was quiet. The cost was real.

FHA did its job. Erica's loan worked exactly as designed. The outcome changed only because attention faded.

That is how silent killers operate—and how disciplined borrowers avoid them.

Chapter 12

From Borrower to Architect: Using FHA Loans to Design Financial Freedom, Not Just Buy Homes

At some point in the FHA journey, a borrower must decide who they are becoming. Up to this point, the focus has been on approval, avoidance of mistakes, and optimization of outcomes. But the most powerful shift happens when borrowers stop reacting to the mortgage process and begin designing their financial future deliberately. FHA loans are often framed as entry-level tools, but when used strategically over time, they can become foundational instruments in a much larger blueprint—one that includes stability, optionality, and long-term freedom.

Most borrowers never reach this stage because they stop at adequacy. They buy the home, make the payments, and settle into routine. There is nothing inherently wrong with that, but adequacy rarely produces freedom. FHA loans were created to expand access, but access alone does not create leverage. Leverage comes from intentional sequencing—how loans are used, exited, reused, and repositioned across a borrower's life. This chapter exists to show how FHA loans fit into a broader financial architecture rather than a single transaction. The first mindset shift required is understanding that borrowing is not a weakness—it is a design choice. FHA loans allow borrowers to control appreciating assets with minimal upfront capital. When combined with disciplined behavior, this creates asymmetric upside. Borrowers who treat FHA as a temporary crutch miss this advantage. Borrowers who treat it as a strategic entry point gain the ability to reallocate cash toward reserves, education, business, or additional assets. FHA loans free capital. What matters is where that capital goes.

Another critical shift is moving from payment thinking to balance-sheet thinking. Many borrowers evaluate success solely by monthly payment comfort. Architects of financial freedom evaluate net worth, equity velocity, and flexibility. An FHA borrower who pays slightly more monthly but preserves liquidity and captures appreciation may outperform a borrower with a lower payment but delayed ownership. The spreadsheet does not lie—but it must be read correctly.

Time is the most underutilized advantage FHA borrowers possess. FHA loans allow earlier market entry. Earlier entry compounds. Appreciation, amortization, and inflation all work quietly in the background. Borrowers who understand this stop obsessing over short-term inefficiencies and focus on long-term positioning. A few hundred dollars per month becomes irrelevant when measured against years of compounding ownership benefits.

Another hallmark of architectural thinking is optionality. FHA borrowers who preserve credit strength, reserves, and equity maintain options. They can refinance, sell, rent, relocate, or leverage without pressure. Borrowers who overextend, extract equity impulsively, or ignore timing constraints reduce options. Financial freedom is not about having one perfect plan—it is about having multiple viable paths at any moment.

Legacy thinking also enters at this stage. FHA loans are often the first rung on the ladder for first-generation homeowners. The decisions made in these early years echo forward. Properties acquired, refinanced, and retained can later become rental income, college funding vehicles, or retirement stability. Borrowers who treat FHA loans as isolated events rarely capture this ripple effect. Those who think generationally do.

Another defining difference between borrowers and architects is documentation and discipline. Architects track numbers. They revisit assumptions annually. They treat mortgages as active components of a system. They understand when to leave well enough alone and when to intervene. FHA loans reward this behavior quietly and consistently.

Importantly, architects are not reckless. They do not chase leverage for ego or speed. They understand risk and build buffers intentionally. FHA loans allow margin for error, but architects do not rely on forgiveness—they rely on foresight. They build resilience first, acceleration second.

This chapter is not suggesting that every FHA borrower must become an investor, landlord, or portfolio builder. Financial freedom looks different for everyone. For some, it is stability and peace of mind. For others, it is expansion and scale. FHA loans can support both paths—but only when borrowers design with intention rather than drift.

The final lesson of this book—and this series—is that FHA loans do not determine outcomes. Borrowers do. FHA is a framework. Inside that framework, decisions compound. Awareness compounds. Discipline compounds. Over time, the borrower becomes more than a participant—they become the architect of their own financial system.

FHA loans open doors. What you build beyond that door is the real story.

How One FHA Loan Became a $410,000 Advantage

Jordan purchased his first home at age 29 using an FHA loan for $265,000. He put down 3.5%, or $9,275. His loan balance after upfront mortgage insurance was $260,400. His mortgage insurance payment was $148 per month. Jordan viewed FHA as a temporary solution, but he treated the loan intentionally from day one.

Over four years, Jordan's home appreciated at an average rate of 4.5% annually, increasing its value to approximately $318,000. His loan balance dropped to $248,000. His equity was now roughly $70,000. His credit score improved from 635 to 715.

Jordan refinanced into a conventional loan, eliminating mortgage insurance and reducing his payment by $230 per month. Instead of upgrading his lifestyle, he saved that amount consistently.

Three years later, Jordan used those savings plus equity from his first home to purchase a small duplex using another FHA loan. He lived in one unit and rented the other. Rental income offset most of his housing cost. His original home continued appreciating.

By year ten, Jordan owned two properties worth a combined $840,000. His total mortgage balance was $430,000. His net equity position was approximately $410,000. He had never earned more than $95,000 per year, never inherited money, and never took extreme risk. The math worked because the strategy was layered. FHA was not the goal—it was the gateway. Jordan did not win because the market was perfect. He won because he treated borrowing as architecture, not desperation.

That is the difference between buying a home and designing freedom.

Chapter 13

The Long Game Advantage: Why FHA Borrowers Who Stay Disciplined Always Win

The final difference between FHA borrowers who merely survive the process and those who thrive long after closing is not intelligence, income, or timing. It is endurance. FHA loans favor borrowers who understand that wealth is not built in moments of excitement, but in long stretches of disciplined consistency. The long game—quiet, methodical, and often unglamorous—is where FHA borrowers gain an advantage that is difficult to replicate through any other lending path. This chapter exists to reframe success not as speed, but as durability.

Many borrowers approach FHA loans with a short-term mindset. They focus on getting approved, closing quickly, and moving on emotionally from the process. Once the keys are in hand, attention fades. But FHA loans are not static. Every month, principal reduces. Every year, equity shifts. Market forces, inflation, and income growth all work in the background. Borrowers who remain aware of these dynamics position themselves to benefit quietly while others drift. One of the most misunderstood aspects of FHA loans is how forgiving time can be. Early inefficiencies—slightly higher rates, mortgage insurance, or modest cash flow pressure—often disappear when measured across a decade. Borrowers who panic early and make reactive changes frequently lock in permanent disadvantages. Borrowers who stay the course allow time to smooth rough edges. FHA loans reward patience paired with vigilance.

Discipline is the engine of the long game. FHA borrowers who succeed resist lifestyle inflation even as their financial position improves. They allow raises, bonuses, and savings to strengthen reserves rather than inflate obligations. This discipline preserves optionality. When refinance opportunities appear, disciplined borrowers qualify easily. When markets soften, they remain solvent. When opportunities arise, they have capacity to act.

Another long-game advantage lies in inflation resistance. Fixed-rate FHA loans lock housing costs while incomes and rents tend to rise over time. Borrowers who hold FHA loans long enough experience a gradual reduction in real housing cost relative to earnings. This silent benefit is rarely discussed, yet it compounds meaningfully over years. Borrowers who abandon ownership too quickly never experience this shift.

Equity growth over time also reshapes borrower psychology. FHA borrowers who hold property through market cycles often reach a point where housing stops feeling risky and starts feeling stabilizing. That psychological shift changes decision-making. Fear diminishes. Planning improves. Borrowers stop reacting and start choosing deliberately. FHA loans are particularly effective at facilitating this transition because they allow earlier entry and longer exposure.

Another critical element of the long game is resisting comparison. Borrowers often judge success against peers who appear to move faster—buying larger homes, refinancing aggressively, or expanding portfolios quickly. FHA borrowers who chase comparison frequently overextend. Those who remain grounded in their own timeline compound steadily. The long game does not reward visibility; it rewards sustainability.

Maintenance of credit discipline is another quiet differentiator. FHA borrowers who keep credit clean after closing preserve leverage. They avoid unnecessary inquiries, maintain utilization discipline, and treat credit as a tool rather than a crutch. Over time, this behavior opens doors—lower rates, faster approvals, and broader options. Credit strength compounds just like equity.

The long game also includes knowing when *not* to act. FHA borrowers who constantly tinker—refinancing repeatedly, extracting equity unnecessarily, or changing terms without clear benefit—often erode gains. Strategic inaction is as important as action. Borrowers who understand this avoid transaction fatigue and preserve momentum.

Perhaps the greatest advantage of the long game is resilience. FHA borrowers who build reserves, protect equity, and maintain flexibility weather disruptions more easily. Job changes, market shifts, and life events do not derail them. They have margin. Margin creates calm. Calm creates better decisions. FHA loans, when paired with discipline, create margin quietly.

This chapter is not about maximizing returns or accelerating growth aggressively. It is about ensuring that progress, once made, is never lost. FHA loans are particularly well-suited for this purpose because they emphasize stability, accessibility, and forgiveness. Borrowers who align with those values outperform through consistency rather than intensity.

The long game is not passive. It is attentive, deliberate, and measured. FHA borrowers who understand this do not look for hacks or shortcuts. They build systems, habits, and awareness that carry them through decades. Over time, those habits matter more than any single decision.

FHA loans do not create overnight success. They create the conditions for lasting success. Borrowers who remain disciplined long enough discover that what once felt like a limitation becomes a foundation.

How Consistency Turned a "Modest" FHA Loan into $287,000

Natalie purchased her home using an FHA loan at age 31 for $295,000. She put down 3.5%, or $10,325. Her loan balance after upfront mortgage insurance was $289,900. Her mortgage insurance payment was $160 per month. At the time, Natalie felt the loan was "good enough," not exceptional.

Natalie made one decision early: she would not rush. She made every payment on time, avoided new debt, and saved modestly. Over the next seven years, her home appreciated at an average of 4% annually, increasing its value to approximately $388,000. Her loan balance dropped to roughly $258,000.

Natalie refinanced into a conventional loan at year seven, eliminating mortgage insurance and lowering her payment by $210 per month. She did not extract equity. She did not upgrade her lifestyle. She simply allowed the system to keep working.

Three years later, her home was worth approximately $435,000. Her loan balance was $246,000. Her equity position was now roughly $189,000.

Including the principal she paid down, appreciation gained, and mortgage insurance she avoided after refinancing, Natalie's FHA loan contributed approximately $287,000 to her net worth over ten years.

Had Natalie rented at $2,100 per month for the same period, she would have spent $252,000 with no asset to show for it. Had she overreacted early and refinanced repeatedly, her costs would have been higher and her equity lower.

Natalie did not win by being aggressive. She won by being consistent.

The math rewarded discipline. Time did the heavy lifting.

That is the long game advantage—and why FHA borrowers who stay disciplined always win.

Chapter 14

The Final Advantage: Mastering FHA So the System Never Controls You

At the end of every borrowing journey lies a simple question: who is in control—the borrower or the system? FHA loans are often misunderstood as rigid, bureaucratic, or limiting, yet the reality is far more nuanced. FHA does not control outcomes. Borrower behavior does. The final advantage FHA borrowers gain is not approval, leverage, or access—it is mastery. Mastery turns rules into tools, constraints into structure, and complexity into clarity. This chapter exists to cement that understanding and close the series with the most important lesson of all: control is learned, not granted.

Most borrowers spend their financial lives reacting. They react to rate changes, lender requests, market headlines, and life events. FHA borrowers who reach mastery stop reacting and start operating. They understand the framework well enough to anticipate outcomes before they occur. They know how underwriters think, how numbers interact, and how timing reshapes options. This knowledge transforms FHA from a program they participate in into a system they navigate confidently. Control begins with understanding cause and effect. Every FHA decision has a consequence, even when that consequence is delayed. Choosing to wait has a cost. Choosing to refinance has a cost. Choosing not to refinance has a cost. Mastery is not about avoiding cost—it is about choosing which costs are worth paying. FHA borrowers who win long-term do not ask whether something is "allowed." They ask whether it aligns with their plan.

Another element of mastery is detachment from fear. FHA borrowers are often told what they *should* worry about—mortgage insurance, credit scores, property standards, or market cycles. Borrowers who never move beyond fear remain stuck in defensive mode. Mastery replaces fear with fluency. When borrowers understand how mortgage insurance works, they stop fearing it. When they understand refinance mechanics, they stop procrastinating. Knowledge does not eliminate risk, but it removes paralysis.

Mastery also involves knowing when to break patterns. Many borrowers repeat the same financial behaviors simply because they are familiar. FHA borrowers who master the system are willing to pause, reassess, and change course when numbers justify it. They understand that refinancing is not failure, selling is not defeat, and holding is not laziness. Each action is a tool to be deployed at the right time, not a judgment on past decisions. Another defining feature of mastery is simplicity. As borrowers become more experienced, they often realize that complexity is rarely necessary. FHA success does not require constant optimization, frequent transactions, or aggressive leverage. It requires consistency, awareness, and selective action. Borrowers who master FHA reduce noise. They focus on a few critical metrics—equity, cash flow, credit strength, and timing—and ignore the rest.

This chapter also marks the transition from learning to teaching, even if only informally. Borrowers who master FHA naturally become resources for others. They explain concepts clearly, dispel myths confidently, and model calm decision-making. This reinforces their own understanding and creates a feedback loop of clarity. Mastery compounds when shared.

Importantly, mastery does not mean perfection. Even the most disciplined FHA borrowers make suboptimal decisions at times. The difference is recovery speed. Masters recognize missteps early and adjust without ego. They do not cling to decisions that no longer serve them. FHA loans allow this adaptability, but only for borrowers willing to reassess honestly.

The final advantage is permanence. FHA borrowers who master the system do not fear the next market shift, job change, or life transition. They have options. Options create calm. Calm creates better decisions. Over time, this stability becomes its own form of wealth. FHA loans were designed to promote stability, but mastery transforms stability into freedom.

As this series closes, remember that FHA is not a loophole, a shortcut, or a compromise. It is a framework. Within that framework, borrowers who learn deeply, act deliberately, and adjust intelligently create outcomes that last decades. The system never controls those borrowers—they control how the system serves them.

That is the final advantage. And it belongs to anyone willing to learn.

The $92,000 Difference Between Reaction and Control

Evan purchased his home using an FHA loan for $315,000 with a 3.5% down payment of $11,025. His loan balance after upfront mortgage insurance was $309,800. His mortgage insurance payment was $170 per month. Evan had two paths in front of him, though he did not realize it at the time.

In the first scenario, Evan reacted. After two years, rates rose, headlines turned negative, and Evan assumed refinancing was no longer an option. He focused only on his payment and ignored equity growth. Over the next five years, he paid

$10,200 in mortgage insurance and missed an opportunity to refinance when his loan-to-value ratio dropped below 80%. In the second scenario—the one Evan eventually chose—he gained control. At year three, his home had appreciated to $355,000, and his loan balance had dropped to $298,000. His equity exceeded 16%. His credit score had improved from 645 to 710. Evan refinanced into a conventional loan, eliminating mortgage insurance and lowering his payment by $215 per month.

Over the next six years, Evan saved $15,480 in eliminated mortgage insurance and approximately $26,500 in reduced interest compared to the original loan path. He redirected those savings into reserves and modest investments. By year nine, the difference between reacting and controlling totaled approximately $92,000.

Nothing dramatic happened. No crisis occurred. Evan simply learned how the system worked—and acted when the math supported it.

The FHA loan did not change. Evan did.

That is mastery. And that is how borrowers ensure the system never controls them.

Chapter 15

Future-Proof Borrowing: How FHA Borrowers Stay Ahead While the Rules, Markets, and Economy Change

One of the greatest misconceptions about FHA loans is that they are static tools governed by fixed rules that never change. In reality, FHA lending exists within a living system—one shaped by economic cycles, policy updates, market behavior, and borrower trends. Borrowers who treat FHA as a one-time rulebook eventually feel blindsided when conditions shift. Borrowers who understand FHA as an adaptive framework remain calm, prepared, and ahead of the curve. This chapter exists to teach future-proof borrowing—the ability to maintain control regardless of how rules, markets, or personal circumstances evolve.

Change is inevitable. Interest rates rise and fall. Housing markets expand and contract. FHA guidelines adjust. Employment landscapes shift. Borrowers who succeed long-term do not predict these changes perfectly; they design resilience into their decisions so that change becomes manageable rather than disruptive. FHA loans, when structured intelligently, allow this resilience by prioritizing accessibility, flexibility, and margin. But margin only exists when borrowers intentionally preserve it.

The first principle of future-proof borrowing is avoiding maximum leverage. FHA allows low down payments and high ratios, but that does not mean borrowers should always use the maximum available. Borrowers who stretch to the edge of approval often leave themselves vulnerable to even small disruptions. Those who stay slightly inside the boundary retain room to maneuver. Future-proof borrowers understand that qualifying is not the same as thriving. They choose sustainability over extremity.

Another key element is liquidity preservation. Cash reserves are the shock absorbers of homeownership. FHA borrowers who drain savings to minimize payments or avoid mortgage insurance often sacrifice the very protection that makes FHA powerful. Markets change faster than borrowers expect. Job transitions, medical expenses, and unexpected repairs arrive without warning. Borrowers who preserve liquidity weather these moments without panic or forced decisions. Liquidity buys time, and time restores control.

Credit stewardship is another pillar of future-proofing. FHA borrowers who maintain clean credit profiles after closing keep access to better options. They avoid unnecessary inquiries, manage utilization carefully, and treat credit as strategic leverage rather than emergency funding. As guidelines evolve and lenders tighten or loosen overlays, borrowers with strong credit profiles remain eligible across programs. Credit strength is adaptability.

Property flexibility also matters. FHA borrowers who choose homes that appeal broadly—rather than narrowly—maintain exit optionality. Homes that are easy to sell, rent, or refinance protect borrowers from being trapped by location, condition, or design. FHA guidelines encourage habitability, but borrowers must think beyond minimum standards. Future-proof borrowers consider how a property will perform across multiple scenarios, not just today's needs.

Another often-overlooked factor is mindset toward policy changes. FHA rules do change, but rarely without warning or rationale. Borrowers who stay informed rather than reactive avoid unnecessary fear. They understand that tightening guidelines usually follow market excess, and easing guidelines often follow contraction. This awareness allows borrowers to plan moves around policy cycles rather than be surprised by them.

Future-proof borrowers also resist the urge to anchor decisions to current conditions. A rate that feels high today may feel low in five years. A payment that feels tight early may feel trivial later. Borrowers who over-optimize for the present often undermine the future. FHA loans reward borrowers who think in phases, understanding that financial comfort evolves over time.

Another hallmark of future-proofing is intentional review. Borrowers who revisit their loan annually—checking balance, equity, credit, and market conditions—spot opportunities early. This habit requires little effort but produces outsized benefit. FHA loans do not require constant action, but they do reward periodic attention.

Importantly, future-proofing does not mean being conservative to the point of stagnation. It means being selective. FHA borrowers who future-proof still take action when the math supports it. They refinance, relocate, or leverage when aligned with long-term goals. The difference is that these actions are planned rather than forced.

The final element of future-proof borrowing is emotional steadiness. Markets amplify emotion—fear during downturns, greed during expansions. FHA borrowers who remain steady make better decisions. They do not rush to sell during volatility or overextend during booms. They understand that FHA loans are designed to support stability, not speculation.

Future-proof FHA borrowers do not need perfect foresight. They need margin, awareness, and adaptability. When those elements are present, change becomes navigable rather than threatening. FHA loans were created to provide stability in uncertain times. Borrowers who future-proof themselves ensure that stability lasts regardless of what comes next.

The $67,400 Cushion That Made the Difference

Rachel purchased her home using an FHA loan for $290,000 with a 3.5% down payment of $10,150. Her loan balance after upfront mortgage insurance was $284,600. Her mortgage insurance payment was $158 per month. At closing, Rachel qualified for a higher loan amount, but she intentionally bought below her maximum approval.

Rachel preserved $18,000 in savings after closing. Over the next three years, her home appreciated to approximately $330,000, and her loan balance dropped to $271,000. Her equity grew steadily, but more importantly, her reserves remained intact.

In year four, Rachel's employer restructured, reducing her income temporarily by $1,200 per month. Many homeowners in similar situations panicked. Rachel did not. She covered the gap using reserves for eight months without missing a payment or accumulating debt.

During that same period, interest rates declined. Rachel's credit score had improved from 640 to 710. Her loan-to-value ratio fell below 82%. She refinanced into a conventional loan, eliminating mortgage insurance and reducing her payment by $245 per month.

Over the next five years, Rachel saved approximately $14,700 in eliminated mortgage insurance and $22,000 in interest compared to staying in the FHA loan. Combined with appreciation and principal reduction, the cushion she preserved early translated into roughly $67,400 in financial advantage.

Had Rachel borrowed to the maximum and drained reserves at closing, she would have faced income disruption with no buffer and missed the refinance window entirely.

The math was simple. Margin created options. Options created control.

That is future-proof borrowing—and why FHA borrowers who plan ahead stay ahead.

Final Thoughts

The Quiet Power of Understanding—and What You Do With It

If there is one truth that echoes through every chapter of this book and across the entire FHA Homeownership & Wealth Series, it is this: outcomes are rarely determined by access alone. Millions of borrowers qualify for FHA loans every year, yet only a fraction use them in ways that meaningfully change their financial trajectory. The difference is not intelligence, luck, or timing. It is understanding—followed by disciplined action over time. FHA loans open the door, but what happens after the door opens is entirely up to the borrower.

Homeownership is often portrayed as a single milestone, a box to be checked, or a symbol of arrival. In reality, it is a system you enter—one that interacts with your income, credit, habits, emotions, and long-term goals. FHA loans were designed to make entry into that system more accessible, especially for borrowers who do not fit traditional molds. That design is not a weakness. It is an invitation. An invitation to participate earlier, learn faster, and compound benefits longer. But invitations can be wasted when misunderstood. Throughout this series, you have seen how myths distort perception, how small mistakes quietly erode outcomes, and how timing reshapes opportunity. You have also seen the opposite: how informed borrowers use FHA loans to stabilize housing costs, preserve liquidity, build equity, and transition deliberately into stronger positions. None of those outcomes happen by accident. They happen when borrowers stop treating FHA as a fallback and start treating it as a framework.

Frameworks matter because they shape behavior. FHA does not promise perfection, but it does reward consistency. It does not eliminate risk, but it allows room to recover. It does not guarantee wealth, but it creates conditions where wealth can grow if nurtured. Borrowers who internalize this stop chasing ideal scenarios and start optimizing real ones. They stop waiting for permission and start managing probabilities.

One of the most powerful shifts a borrower can make is moving from a transaction mindset to a stewardship mindset. Transactions end. Stewardship continues. FHA borrowers who view their mortgage as something to be managed rather than escaped begin to see options everywhere—refinance windows, equity strategies, rental potential, geographic flexibility, and long-term stability. This mindset replaces urgency with patience and replaces fear with fluency.

Another lesson reinforced repeatedly is that simplicity often outperforms complexity. FHA success does not require constant movement, aggressive leverage, or perfect forecasting. It requires awareness, restraint, and periodic recalibration. Borrowers who check in with their numbers annually—loan balance, equity, credit, market conditions—almost always outperform those who "set it and forget it." Attention is a form of leverage, and it costs nothing.

This series has also made clear that FHA loans are not just financial tools—they are behavioral mirrors. They reflect how borrowers handle discipline, delayed gratification, risk, and change. Borrowers who use FHA well tend to develop stronger financial habits overall. They become more intentional, more patient, and more confident in decision-making. These traits extend beyond housing and influence every area of financial life.

It is also important to recognize that success does not look the same for everyone. For some borrowers, success is stability—knowing the payment is fixed, the home is safe, and the future is predictable. For others, success is flexibility—the ability to move, invest, or expand. FHA loans can support both paths when used intentionally. The mistake is assuming there is one correct outcome. The goal is alignment, not imitation.

As markets evolve and policies change, the principles you have learned here remain durable. Preserve margin. Respect leverage. Track timing. Protect credit. Plan exits. Stay adaptable. These ideas are not tied to a single rate environment or housing cycle. They are portable. Borrowers who internalize them remain effective regardless of external conditions.

If there is a quiet warning embedded in these final thoughts, it is this: do not underestimate the cost of inattention. FHA loans rarely harm borrowers dramatically. They harm them subtly—through overpayment, delay, drift, and missed opportunity. Those costs accumulate silently until years have passed. Awareness is the antidote. Even modest attention, applied consistently, prevents most negative outcomes.

Equally important is recognizing that no single decision defines success. Borrowers often fixate on whether they made the "right" choice at one moment—buying now versus later, refinancing versus waiting, selling versus holding. In truth, success is cumulative. A reasonable decision, followed by good habits, often outperforms a perfect decision followed by neglect. FHA loans give borrowers time to learn and adjust. Use that time.

As this book closes, remember that mastery is not about

memorizing rules. It is about understanding relationships—between debt and cash flow, equity and flexibility, time and compounding. When those relationships are clear, decisions become calmer and outcomes more predictable. FHA stops being intimidating and starts being navigable.

The ultimate purpose of this series was never to convince you that FHA loans are superior to all others. It was to show you that when FHA loans are chosen consciously and managed deliberately, they can be transformative. They allow everyday borrowers to participate in ownership, stability, and long-term growth without waiting for ideal conditions that may never arrive.

What happens next is not dictated by this book, the program, or the market. It is dictated by how you apply what you now understand. Whether you buy your first home, refinance thoughtfully, build equity patiently, or simply sleep better knowing you are in control, the advantage you carry forward is clarity.

Clarity compounds. And when paired with discipline, it quietly changes everything.

That is the real wealth FHA loans can help build—and it lasts far beyond the loan itself.

The FHA Homeownership & Wealth Series

Complete Roadmap: From First-Time Buyer to Long-Term Wealth Builder

The FHA Homeownership & Wealth Series is designed as a progressive journey. Each book builds on the previous one, guiding borrowers from basic understanding to confident ownership, strategic financing, and long-term wealth creation. Readers can enter at any stage, but those who follow the full roadmap gain the clearest, fastest path to results.

This series is structured to meet borrowers exactly where they are—and show them what comes next.

Phase 1: Foundation & Confidence (Books 1–3)

Understanding FHA and realizing you qualify

These books eliminate confusion, fear, and misinformation. They are designed to answer the most important early question: *Is homeownership actually possible for me?*

Book 1 – FHA Loans Explained for Beginners How FHA Mortgages Work, Who Qualifies, and Why They're One of the Easiest Paths to Homeownership This is the foundation of the entire series. Readers learn how FHA loans work, why they exist, and how to evaluate FHA realistically using math instead of myths. This book builds confidence and replaces hesitation with clarity.

Book 2 – Buying Your First Home with FHA A Step-by-Step Guide to Purchasing a Home with Low Down Payment and Flexible Credit Rules This book turns understanding into action. Readers learn the full buying process—from pre-approval to closing—so they know exactly what to expect and how to avoid common first-time buyer mistakes.

Book 3 – FHA Loans for Borrowers with Low Credit or Past Credit Issues How to Get Approved with FHA Even with Late Payments, Collections, or a Low Credit Score This book is for borrowers who believe their credit disqualifies them. It explains FHA's second-chance philosophy and shows how recovery, not perfection, determines approval.

Phase 2: Income Reality & Property Flexibility (Books 4–6)

Qualifying with real-life finances and real homes

These books expand what readers believe is possible by addressing income types, property types, and cash requirements.

Book 4 – FHA Loans for Self-Employed, 1099 & Gig Workers How Business Owners and Independent Contractors Qualify for FHA Home Loans This book demystifies income calculations for non-traditional earners and shows how FHA accommodates modern work patterns.

Book 5 – FHA Loans for Fixer-Uppers, Condos & Non-Perfect Homes How to Buy Homes That Need Repairs or Don't Fit Traditional Loan Guidelines Readers learn how FHA views property condition and how renovation and condo options expand buying opportunities.

Book 6 – FHA Loan Limits, Down Payment & Closing Costs How Much You Can Borrow and How to Bring Less Money to the Closing Table This book focuses on numbers. Readers learn how FHA loan limits work, how to reduce cash to close, and how seller credits and assistance programs change affordability.

Phase 3: Optimization & Refinancing Strategy (Books 7–8)

Using FHA beyond the purchase

These books show how FHA loans evolve with the borrower.

Book 7 – FHA Refinance Options Made Simple Streamline, Rate-and-Term, and Cash-Out Refinancing Explained for Homeowners Readers learn how FHA supports refinancing, payment reduction, and financial repositioning over time.

Book 8 – Using an FHA Cash-Out Refinance to Build Wealth How to Turn Home Equity into Cash Without Selling Your Home This book introduces equity as a strategic tool, not just a number on paper, while emphasizing responsible use.

Phase 4: Income & Expansion (Books 9–10)

Turning ownership into leverage

These books shift the reader from homeowner to strategist.

Book 9 – Buying Multi-Unit Homes with FHA How to Purchase 2–4 Unit Properties, Live in One, and Rent the Rest Readers learn how FHA enables owner-occupied investing and rent-offset strategies that dramatically reduce housing costs.

Book 10 – FHA Loan Myths, Mistakes & Borrower Strategies What Most Buyers Get Wrong—and How Smart Borrowers Win with FHA Loans This is the strategic wrap-up book that reinforces best practices, avoids costly errors, and helps readers think like informed borrowers.

About the Author

Joe Correa is a mortgage professional, educator, and financial strategist dedicated to helping everyday people understand homeownership, credit, and wealth-building without confusion or intimidation. With years of hands-on experience in the mortgage industry, Joe has worked with first-time buyers, self-employed borrowers, credit-challenged families, and aspiring investors who were often told "no" before learning what was actually possible.

What sets Joe apart is his ability to translate complex lending rules into clear, practical guidance. Rather than relying on theory, his work is grounded in real-world scenarios, real numbers, and real borrower outcomes. He believes that most people do not fail to buy homes because they lack income or discipline, but because they lack accurate information. His mission is to replace myths with math and fear with understanding.

Joe specializes in FHA loans because he has seen firsthand how transformative they can be when used correctly. He views FHA not as a last resort, but as one of the most powerful entry points into homeownership and long-term wealth—especially for borrowers navigating modern financial realities such as student loans, variable income, credit recovery, or limited savings. Through his writing, Joe teaches borrowers how to think strategically, act confidently, and use lending tools intentionally rather than emotionally.

In addition to his mortgage work, Joe is the creator of multiple educational programs and book series focused on homeownership, credit building, refinancing strategies, and financial independence. His approach emphasizes sustainability over speculation and progress over perfection. He is known for breaking down decisions into simple frameworks that empower readers to make smart choices at every stage of their journey.

Joe's writing style reflects his core belief: financial education should be accessible, practical, and empowering. He does not promise shortcuts or hype outcomes. Instead, he provides clarity, structure, and realistic paths forward—so readers can move from uncertainty to ownership with confidence.

When he is not writing or working with borrowers, Joe continues developing educational resources designed to help families build stability, equity, and long-term opportunity through informed financial decisions.

How to Get a Personalized FHA Review

If you found this book helpful, you may want to see how FHA loan options apply to your specific income, credit profile, cash to close, and homeownership goals.

Every borrower's situation is different. FHA guidelines, loan limits, interest rates, mortgage insurance, and available options vary based on income type, credit history, debt levels, savings, property type, and state guidelines. The examples in this book are educational, but your personal FHA eligibility, payment range, and strategy can only be determined through an individualized review.

As a licensed mortgage broker, I offer a **Personalized FHA Review** designed to show you: • Whether you currently qualify for an FHA loan • Your realistic home price and monthly payment range • How much cash you may need for down payment and closing costs • How credit, debt, or income factors affect your approval • Whether FHA is the best option for you now or later • What steps, if any, would strengthen your position

This review is fast, confidential, and focused entirely on helping you make informed homeownership decisions—without pressure or obligation.

To request your personalized FHA review, visit:https://finibimortgage.carrd.co/

You may also submit your information through the QR code provided in this book.

Your financial profile already tells a story.This review shows you how FHA lenders will read it.

Yours truly,

Joseph G. Correa

Licensed Mortgage Broker, Finibi Mortgage

Educational & Financial Disclaimer

This book is provided for educational and informational purposes only. The content is intended to help readers better understand FHA loans, homeownership concepts, and general mortgage strategies, but it does not constitute financial advice, legal advice, tax advice, or lending approval. Mortgage guidelines, FHA requirements, interest rates, loan programs, and qualification standards are subject to change and may vary based on individual circumstances, lender overlays, geographic location, and market conditions.

Nothing in this book should be interpreted as a guarantee of loan approval, loan terms, interest rates, or eligibility. All examples, scenarios, calculations, and illustrations are for educational purposes only and are not intended to represent actual loan offers or outcomes. Individual results will vary based on credit profile, income stability, debt obligations, assets, property characteristics, and lender-specific requirements.

Readers are encouraged to consult with a licensed mortgage professional, financial advisor, tax professional, or legal advisor before making any financial or real estate decisions. This book does not replace personalized advice or professional review. Any decisions made based on the information in this book are the sole responsibility of the reader.

The author and publisher are not responsible for any actions taken by readers as a result of the information provided in this book. While every effort has been made to ensure accuracy at the time of publication, no representation or warranty is made regarding the completeness, reliability, or current applicability of the information contained herein.

By reading this book, you acknowledge that homeownership and mortgage decisions involve risk and personal responsibility, and you agree that the author and publisher are not liable for any financial outcomes, losses, or damages that may result from reliance on this material.

This book is designed to educate, not to instruct or advise on individual financial decisions. Its purpose is to provide general understanding so readers can ask better questions, seek appropriate professional guidance, and make informed choices based on their unique circumstances.

Risk Disclosure

Homeownership and mortgage financing involve financial risk. While FHA loans are designed to increase access to homeownership and provide flexible qualification standards, they do not eliminate risk, and outcomes may vary based on individual circumstances, market conditions, and personal financial decisions. Purchasing or refinancing a home requires a long-term financial commitment and should be evaluated carefully.

Housing markets can fluctuate. Property values may increase or decrease over time, and there is no guarantee that a home will appreciate in value. Economic conditions, interest rate changes, local market factors, and unforeseen events can affect property values, mortgage payments, and resale opportunities. Borrowers should be prepared for the possibility that home values may remain flat or decline during certain periods.

Mortgage payments represent a fixed obligation that must be met regardless of changes in income, employment status, health, or personal circumstances. Failure to make mortgage payments may result in late fees, credit damage, default, or foreclosure. Borrowers should ensure they have adequate income stability, savings, and contingency planning before entering into any mortgage obligation. FHA loans include mortgage insurance, which increases the total cost of borrowing. While mortgage insurance enables access to lower down payments and more flexible credit standards, it may remain in place for a significant portion of the loan term unless refinanced or otherwise removed under applicable guidelines. Borrowers should understand how mortgage insurance affects monthly payments and long-term costs.

Refinancing, selling, or leveraging home equity is not guaranteed to be available in the future. These options depend on market conditions, interest rates, credit profile, equity levels, and lender requirements at the time of action. Borrowers should not assume future refinancing opportunities or equity access when making initial homeownership decisions.

Rental income, including income from multi-unit properties or converted rentals, is not guaranteed. Vacancies, maintenance costs, market conditions, tenant behavior, and regulatory changes can impact rental cash flow. Borrowers considering rental strategies should evaluate these risks carefully and avoid relying on projected rental income for financial stability.

This book does not provide investment advice or predict financial outcomes. All examples and scenarios are illustrative only and should not be relied upon as forecasts or guarantees.

Readers are responsible for conducting their own due diligence and seeking professional advice when appropriate.

By choosing to pursue homeownership or mortgage financing, readers acknowledge the presence of risk and accept responsibility for their financial decisions. The author and publisher are not responsible for any losses, damages, or adverse outcomes resulting from actions taken based on the information provided in this book.

This disclosure is intended to promote informed decision-making, not discourage homeownership. Understanding risk is a critical part of using FHA loans responsibly and sustainably.

www.ingramcontent.com/pod-product-compliance
Ingram Content Group UK Ltd.
Pitfield, Milton Keynes, MK11 3LW, UK
UKHW020158290926
15471UKWH00005B/943

9 798295 619694